Nellie Bly's Monkey

NELLIE BLY'S MONKEY

MONKEY

His Remarkable Story in His Own Words

by Joan W. Blos
illustrated by Catherine Stock

MORROW JUNIOR BOOKS
NEW YORK

Introduction

When Nellie Bly suggested a trip around the world, her editors at *The World*, New York's famous newspaper, were extremely doubtful. They didn't think it proper—or safe—for so young a woman to travel so far alone. Also, they didn't believe she could do it as quickly as she promised.

Those were the days of railroad trains and steamships and horse-drawn carriages. Merely to go from New York to Chicago, using the very best of trains, took two full days and nights! So how could she possibly go around the world in *seventy-five days,* or even less, which is what she proposed? And what about her luggage? Female travelers were not known to travel light. With all the luggage she would surely require, how would she avoid delays when making needed connections?

Nellie met all of their arguments and added a few of her own.

They decided to let her try.

On November 14, 1889, Nellie Bly appeared at the dock with a small but well-packed satchel. It contained writing supplies and a few personal items, such as a nightgown and some undergarments. Throughout her entire journey she would wear what she had on that day: a specially tailored blue serge dress, checked coat, and gillie hat. On her right thumb she wore her lucky ring, and she carried two watches: one to remain on New York time, one to reset along the way to agree with local time.

Headlines in *The World* announced the dramatic beginning of Nellie Bly's adventure. Thereafter her telegraphed stories were immediately published all across the country; invented games and competitions also served to keep her adventure in the public mind. On January 25, three days ahead of schedule, Nellie Bly was home.

Suddenly she was famous! It wasn't long before her book about the trip was a national best-seller. Reading the final chapters of *Nellie Bly's Book: Around the World in 72 Days,* one finds lively descriptions of the last parts of her journey and the crowds that cheered her as she crossed the country. There are also scattered mentions of a small, irresistible monkey purchased in Singapore.

I have taken the liberty of elaborating the story of that monkey, and I have chosen to do so "in his own words."

—J.W.B.

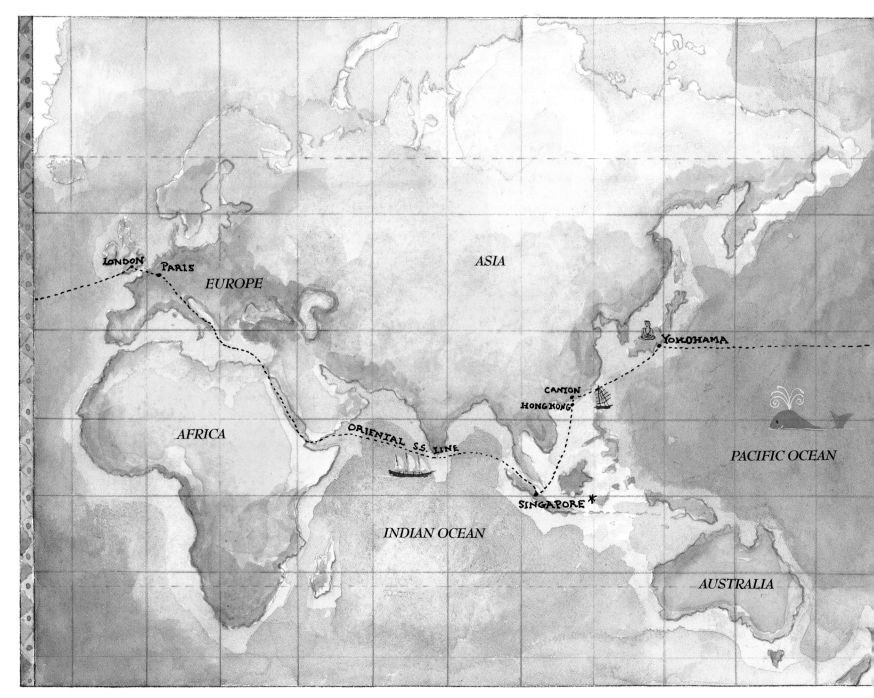

LONDON
PARIS
EUROPE
ASIA
AFRICA
ORIENTAL S.S. LINE
YOKOHAMA
CANTON
HONG KONG
SINGAPORE *
INDIAN OCEAN
PACIFIC OCEAN
AUSTRALIA

* Where I met Nellie Bly

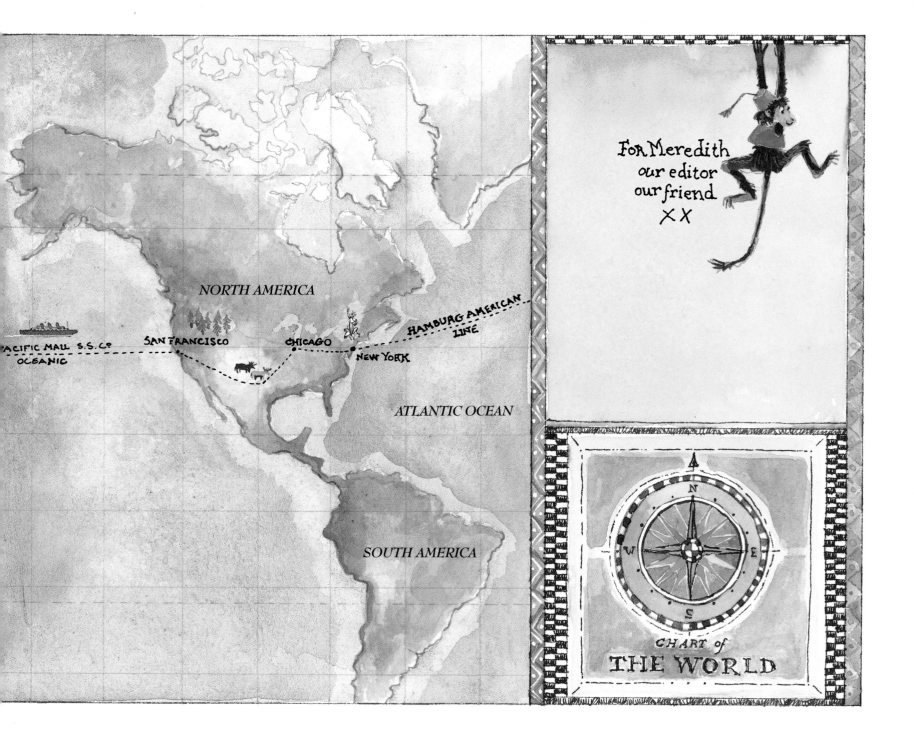

For Meredith
our editor
our friend
X X

NORTH AMERICA

ATLANTIC OCEAN

SOUTH AMERICA

PACIFIC MAIL S.S.Cº
OCEANIC

SAN FRANCISCO

CHICAGO

NEW YORK

HAMBURG AMERICAN
LINE

N

W E

S

CHART of
THE WORLD

In Which I Leave My Home

No one remembered, or told me, exactly where I was born. I was captured at an early age and promptly taken to Singapore by my new Malaysian master. He was a driver of hired carriages and had to work long hours to support his family. Although I was treated well enough, certain important matters were never understood. For example, we monkeys are curious by nature. Yet I, a curious youngster, was confined to the house and yard.

Forbidden to set my feet upon the road, I filled my mind with rare and extravagant stories of the travelers I observed.

On a day I shall always remember, my master returned unexpectedly, and a foreign lady stepped down. This brave American lady was named Miss Nellie Bly. It was her intention to travel all around the world and to do so faster than had ever been done before. "Yes," my master explained to us. "She is telling about this thing in the newspapers of her country!"

My master said he had spoken well of me—my good disposition and cleverness—and the American lady wished to make my acquaintance.

"It is more than that," she corrected. "Please say that my journey has taken me far from home. I am therefore lonely and wish to buy the monkey. My entire happiness now depends on him."

Seven coins persuaded my master.

No sooner were they counted out than he patted me lightly on my head, wished the two of us good luck, and gave me to my new owner.

Just before we started off, the smallest daughter removed the silver chain she wore and held it out to me. Knowing that I should miss her, I put the pretty thing on.

A Race with Time Declared

Early the next morning we boarded the *Oriental*. A five-day voyage would take us to Hong Kong, port city of British China. There we would stay, with the boat as our hotel, while awaiting the arrival of the other passengers.

```
┌──────────────────────────────────────────────────┐
│   PACIFIC UNION CABLE                              │
│   ─────────────────────────────────────           │
│                                                    │
│   ┌─────────┐                                      │
│   │TO AGENT │                                       │
│   ├─────────┴──────────────────┐                   │
│   │O & O SHIPPING COMPANY       │                  │
│   ├──────────┐                  │                  │
│   │HONG KONG │                                      │
│   └──────────┘                                      │
│                                                    │
│   ┌──────────────────┐┌──────────────┐┌──────────┐│
│   │APPRECIATE EFFORTS ON││BEHALF MISS ││BISLAND STOP││
│   └──────────────────┘└──────────────┘└──────────┘│
│                          ┌────────┐┌────────┐      │
│                          │[SIGNED]││ JOURNAL│      │
│                          └────────┘└────────┘      │
└──────────────────────────────────────────────────┘
```

We were delighted to reach our destination sooner than expected. My mistress then hurried to the shipping company's office, hoping for letters from home. Instead the agent told her that another American lady, also a reporter, was also circling the globe!

"Not only that," our informant went on to say, "this Miss Elizabeth Bisland has just passed through our city. She vows to complete the journey more quickly than yourself!"

"But I am racing with Time alone," my mistress proudly declared. "If someone travels faster than I, it is no concern of mine."

We returned to our cabin directly. Once there my mistress spread out her map and traced our route with her finger. As she named the cities still to be reached—Yokohama and San Francisco, Chicago and New York—I was suddenly overcome with longing for my home.

That night, in an effort to cheer us both, my mistress divided her meal with me. Later, a pillow beside her bed provided a place to sleep.

It was then a new thought struck me: If this Miss Bisland reached New York City first, she, and not my mistress, would win the race with Time.

In the Orient

We awoke in better spirits. Our competitor all but forgotten, we resolved to enjoy Hong Kong! It would not be difficult.

The city was new to both of us and with its terraced houses resembled neither Singapore nor the brick and pavement island of Manhattan my mistress described as home.

Spicy foods enticed us with their tangy odors. Vendors called out loudly, and my mistress paused, delighted, at the sight of a wedding party.

As visitors to a foreign land we drew closer together. It was here that she dubbed me McGinty, which has been my name ever since.

On Christmas Day my mistress and I traveled by boat to Canton. At the sight of my first American flag, I took off my little cap, and as I'd seen an American gentleman do, I held it over my heart.

We returned to Hong Kong the next morning. Two days later we received the news that our ship was ready to sail! We said farewell to friends we had made and to British China.

Yokohama was next!

My mistress thoroughly enjoyed Japan and admired the Japanese people. Sorely tired of her practical blue dress, she envied the Japanese women in their bright kimonos.

Although we were eager to be on our way, side trips and other diversions helped us pass the time.

Onward to San Francisco!

As we boarded the *Oceanic,* a ship that carried the Pacific mail and some few passengers, the captain welcomed us warmly.

"All going well," he promised. "We should complete the crossing in just fifteen days!"

But three days later, as the *Oceanic* floundered in high Pacific seas, a cry went up from the superstitious sailors: "Throw the monkey overboard! The monkey has brought bad luck!"

To my lasting gratitude, my mistress boldly snatched me up and carried me to safety. Thereafter I stayed out of sight.

America at Last

Mishaps and misunderstandings awaited in San Francisco.

First, it was feared that the ship's bill of health had been left behind. Without it we passengers could not disembark, and a two-week delay was threatened! On hearing this, my mistress fell into despair.

A few minutes later the bill of health was found and, with relief, we boarded the landing tug.

No sooner had it pulled away than the doctor appeared at the railing. "Stop! Stop! Stop! Return at once!" he shouted to my mistress. "I must examine your tongue!"

By way of an answer, she stuck it out at him, and I followed her example.

Finally, when we reached the pier, we were greeted with the news that a sudden blizzard had closed all railroad traffic over the Rocky Mountains.

Luckily a private train had been arranged by *The World*. It would take a southerly route and thus avoid the snow.

"McGinty," said my mistress, gratefully touching her lucky ring, "it's been quite a day!"

As our train crossed the open prairie, numbers of real cowboys paused to wave to us.

At each station and station stop everyone was singing "My Nellie's Blue Eyes" as hands and handkerchiefs fluttered.

Our train being small, the engine had little to pull. Therefore we traveled swiftly, making many a record-breaking run, especially in Kansas, where the land is flat.

More and more often my mistress spoke of home. Smilingly she described to me the terrier and the parrot that awaited our return.

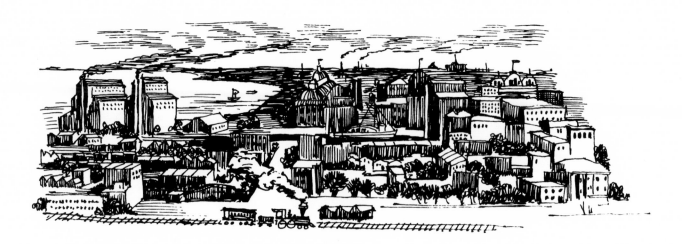

I shall always remember Chicago as the kindest, liveliest, and handsomest of cities. Due to our early arrival, arrangements to entertain us had to be hastily made. Nevertheless the Press Club turned out to greet us, and we breakfasted well at Kinsley's, an excellent restaurant.

At Chicago's Board of Trade the brokers cheered us loudly when my mistress was recognized. Too soon we were driven to Pennsylvania Station, where we boarded the regular train.

As my mistress was later to write, she felt at home in Chicago and wished she could stay all day.

In Ohio and Pennsylvania, steel mills reminded my mistress of the factory workers and mill hands of whom she had often written.

"McGinty," she scolded as I helped myself to a chocolate, "it is time for you to consider that there is more to America than candy, fruit, and flowers."

Soon we were crossing wide and beautiful rivers, equally remarkable for their long and beautiful names. And before you could say "Susquehanna" we arrived in Philadelphia, where an escort of newsmen came aboard the train for the last part of the journey.

My mistress had sailed from a Hoboken pier on November 14, 1889, at 9:40 in the morning. On January 25, 1890, at 3:51 in the afternoon, our train arrived at the Jersey City station and my mistress jumped to the platform.

Amid cheers so loud he could hardly be heard, Jersey City's mayor declared, "The American girl can no longer be misunderstood. She will be recognized as determined, independent, able to take care of herself wherever she may go."

In a welcome described by *The World* the next day, friends and family surrounded her.

Nellie Bly was home.

My New Life Begins

My mistress lived in New York City, in something called an apartment, which is part of a larger house. The house itself was called 120 West 35th Street.

It was there I met the terrier and the parrot of which I had heard so much. My mistress was fond of both of them, but they did not get along. I truly think that in their entire lives the only matter on which these two agreed was their dislike of me. Together they often provoked me. I took to throwing things.

"Do come," my mistress wrote to a friend, "before the monkey knocks the life out of the parrot and the dog shakes the impishness out of the monkey for not one is congenial and friendly with the other and they are in a constant state of hostilities which may break forth at any moment."

I Become a Celebrity!

Shortly thereafter my mistress took me to visit the New York Menagerie, a splendid collection of animals both native and exotic.

Children reached out to offer me roasted chestnuts and pretzels thick with salt. Three small sisters brought to mind my master's little daughters in far-off Singapore.

As we paced the sunny pathways, my mistress explained that arrangements had been made whereby I was to take up residence at the Menagerie. She would visit me often, she promised; neither of us would ever forget the adventures we had shared.

Assured that my mistress would remain my friend, I became quite curious about the plan she proposed. Is not this trait essential to a monkey's nature? I have always said this is so.

I am busiest on Saturdays but can rest on Sundays, when the Menagerie is closed. For the remainder of the week I attend to my own affairs and enjoy the company of my fellow monkeys. Of course, we are always glad to perform for those who come to see us.

My mistress is writing for her newspaper again, but still she visits me often. On such occasions, I am glad to say, she leaves at home that hateful little dog and that noisome bird.

She is faithful in bringing me delicate pieces of fruit—in season, ripe bananas.

It is my pleasure to share them.

For Those Who Wish to Know More

Elizabeth Jane Cochrane was Nellie Bly's real name. Although sometimes claiming a later date, she was born in 1864 in the small Pennsylvania town that had been named for her father, and she died in New York City in 1922. Her career as a reporter began in 1885, when luck and determination led her to a job with the *Pittsburg Dispatch*. (The final *h* was not added to the city name until the twentieth century was well under way.)

It wasn't long before Nellie Bly, her pen name inspired by a Stephen Foster song, was writing bylined stories. She was a clever interviewer, and her good, if uncritical, articles on industrial Pittsburgh, and especially the lives of its working girls, earned appreciative readers. However, as a female reporter she was often assigned to cover bland events, such as flower shows. Bored and impatient after less than a year on the job, Nellie left her position with the *Dispatch* for a trip to Mexico. She stayed six months and, in the first of the four books she would write, told about her travels.

Nellie Bly moved to New York City in 1887. Three months later, against all odds, she obtained a reporter's job with Joseph Pulitzer's newspaper. To fulfill her first assignment for *The World,* she pretended to be mentally ill, then spent ten days as a "patient" in an insane asylum. This strategy worked so well for Nellie that later, in order to expose an employment agency that exploited immigrant women, she convincingly pretended that she was looking for work. Later still she tricked an Albany politician into accepting a bribe. Although personal letters refer to bouts of depression, these moods were not made public. In print Nellie Bly was sassy, chauvinistic, opinionated, and pert.

A second life, and a new career, began in 1895 with marriage to Robert Seaman, a wealthy businessman many years older than Nellie. The workings of his Brooklyn, New York, factory interested her, and she soon joined him in the management of its day-by-day operation. After her husband's death, in 1904, she attempted to run it as an exemplary model of labor-management relations. Unfortunately, this was not successful, and in many ways the last years of her life were difficult and unhappy.

Regarding her career as a "female reporter," it is noteworthy that Nellie Bly frequently chose to write about persons unfairly treated by the social system. In 1888, just a year before her celebrated trip around the world, she gave just coverage to Belva Lockwood's campaign for the presidency. A few years later, although she disagreed with her subject's anarchist viewpoint, she interviewed Emma Goldman sympathetically and at length.

Nellie Bly's story has been told repeatedly as juvenile nonfiction. But readers should exercise caution: Some popular anecdotes cannot be validated. The one authoritative work is Brooke Kroeger's 1994 biography, *Nellie Bly: Daredevil, Reporter, Feminist.* I am indebted to the book for welcome support of research I conducted prior to its publication, to its author for pertinent comments, and to both for the name of the monkey!

Watercolors were used for the full-color illustrations.
The text type is 14-point Bernard Modern Bold.

Text copyright © 1996 by Joan W. Blos
Illustrations copyright © 1996 by Catherine Stock

Printed in Hong Kong by South China Printing Company (1988) Ltd.

1   2   3   4   5   6   7   8   9   10

Library of Congress Cataloging-in-Publication Data
Blos, Joan W.
Nellie Bly's monkey: his remarkable story in his own words/by Joan W. Blos; illustrated by Catherine Stock.
p. cm.
Summary: McGinty the monkey and his new owner, a woman journalist, travel from Singapore to New York,
where he finally takes up residence at the Menagerie.
ISBN 0-688-12677-4 (trade)—ISBN 0-688-12678-2 (library)
1. Bly, Nellie, 1864–1922—Juvenile Fiction.   2. Monkeys—Juvenile Fiction.   [1. Bly, Nellie, 1864–1922—Fiction.
2. Monkeys—Fiction.   3. Journalists—Fiction.   4. Voyages and travels—Fiction.]   I. Stock, Catherine, ill.
II. Title.   PZ10.3.B6216Ne 1996   [E]—dc20   95-13713   CIP AC